The State of Food Insecurity in Gaborone, Botswana

Benjamin Acquah, Stephen Kapunda, Alexander Legwegoh, Thando Gwebu, Tirelo Modie-Moroka, Kesitegile Gobotswang and Aloysius Mosha

Series Editor: Prof. Jonathan Crush

ACKNOWLEDGEMENTS

The important contribution of the African Food Security Urban Network (www.afsun.org) city partners to the design and implementation of the survey in Gaborone is gratefully acknowledged. Bruce Frayne managed the surveys and Wade Pendleton assisted with all aspects of content, design, methodology and analysis. He also undertook the training of field enumerators in Gaborone. The data entry and management was undertaken by Christa Schier and her team at the University of Namibia. Jonathan Crush provided extensive advice and assistance in the writing up of the report. The Food and Nutrition Technical Assistance Project (FANTA) is gratefully acknowledged for providing the methodology and questions used in this survey to collect food insecurity data. The research was funded by the Canadian International Development Agency (CIDA) under its University Partners in Cooperation and Development (UPCD) Tier One Program.

AFSUN

© AFSUN 2013

Published by the African Food Security Urban Network (AFSUN)
African Centre for Cities, University of Cape Town, Private Bag X3
Rondebosch 7701, South Africa
www.afsun.org

First published 2013

ISBN 978-1-920597-08-5

Cover photograph by Alexander Legwegoh

Production by Bronwen Dachs Müller, Cape Town

AUTHORS

Benjamin Acquah is a Senior Lecturer, Department of Economics, University of Botswana.

Stephen Kapunda is an Associate Professor, Department of Economics, University of Botswana.

Alexander Legwegoh is a Postdoctoral Fellow, Department of Geography, University of Guelph.

Thando Gwebu is Professor, Department of Environmental Sciences. University of Botswana.

Tirelo Modie-Moroka is a Senior Lecturer, Department of Social Work, University of Botswana.

Kesitegile Gobotswang was a Senior Lecturer, Department of Family and Consumer Sciences, University of Botswana.

Aloysius Mosha is Professor, Department of Architecture and Planning, University of Botswana.

Previous Publications in the AFSUN Series

CONTENTS

TABLES

FIGURES

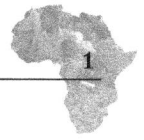

1. Introduction

Botswana has had high and sustained rates of economic growth for the past five decades and is generally considered to be one the best economic performers in Sub-Saharan Africa.[1] Real GDP per capita grew at an average annual rate of 4.4% between 1980 and 2010. The last decade has also seen a significant fall in the incidence of poverty, with the absolute number of persons living below the poverty line declining from around 500,000 in 2002/2003 to about 373,000 in 2009/2010. Despite these positive economic indicators, many development challenges remain.[2] For example, unemployment levels have remained stubbornly high, the incidence of urban poverty has increased over the last decade and income inequality is growing.[3] Middle-income households (those between percentiles 15 and 75) experienced much more rapid income growth over the last decade than those in the lowest 15 percent.[4] As a result, Botswana has one of the highest levels of inequality in Sub-Saharan Africa.[5]

This report examines how Botswana's positive record of economic growth and negative outcomes of growing inequality have affected the food security of the urban poor.[6] While research on food security in Botswana has been undertaken since the 1970s, it has tended to focus on the country's rural areas.[7] In the wake of Botswana's devastating HIV and AIDS epidemic, there has been a concerted research and policy focus on the relationship between the epidemic and food insecurity.[8] But, again, the primary focus has been on the rural areas and the impacts on household agricultural production, despite evidence that HIV prevalence is higher in urban than rural areas.[9] This is consistent with a broader research trend: knowledge about urban food security in Botswana is limited and little is known about the extent and nature of food insecurity in its cities and towns. This makes it difficult for development practitioners and policy makers to quantify the challenge and make plans to reduce the food gap that exists in urban areas.

The Botswana example has wider importance for the general study of urban food security in Africa. First, Botswana is one of the most rapidly urbanizing and most urbanized countries in Africa (second only to South Africa in the Southern African region). Between independence in 1966 and 2001, the proportion of the population living in urban areas increased from 5% to 54% (Table 1). By 2011, the urban population had increased again to 61%. Projections of urban growth suggest that Botswana will be 69% urbanized by 2025 (Figure 1). The percentage of the national population residing in Gaborone and its adjacent satellite communities grew from 15% in 1981 to 26% in 2001 and 25% in 2011. Given that

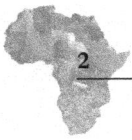

Botswana is further along the urban transition than other African countries, its experience can help illuminate what urban food security challenges others will face in due course.

TABLE 1: Growth of Population in Urban Settlements: 1964–2001						
	1964	1971	1981	1991	2001	2011
No. of urban places	3	5	8	25	34	n/a
Total urban	20,989	54,300	166,400	600,100	909,800	1,243,320
Total population	57,494	596,900	941,000	1,326,800	1,680,900	2,038,228
% urban	3.8	9.1	17.7	45.2	54.1	61.0
Source: Central Statistics Office						

FIGURE 1: Urban Population of Botswana

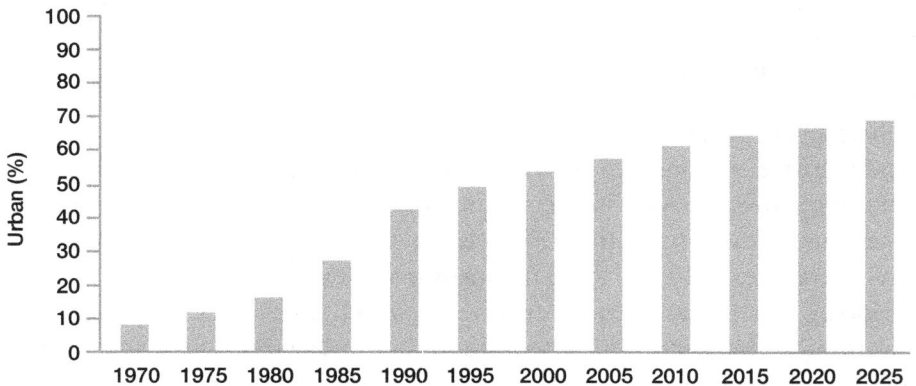

Source: Population Division of the Department of Economic and Social Affairs of the United Nations Secretariat, World Population Prospects: The 2010 Revision.

Second, the notion of food sovereignty is gaining increasing attention in Africa, following the adoption of the Nyéléni Declaration by the Forum for Food Sovereignty in Mali in 2007.[10] Botswana's semi-arid environment, compounded by climate change, means that the country is unlikely ever to be self-sufficient in food even if its youth and rural population were interested in growing it.[11] Of Botswana's total land area of 582,000km^2, crop agriculture is confined to a relatively small area, estimated to be between 2,500km^2 and 3,800km^2 on the eastern and northern margins of the country. Less than one percent of the arable land is cropped (with mostly sorghum, maize, millet and watermelons grown). Productivity is low and, although at independence Botswana aspired to be self-sufficient in food, the country has abandoned this agenda, which has been recognized as largely unachievable.[12] For example, the Accelerated Rainfed Arable Programme (ARAP) provided farmers with ploughing and plant-

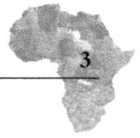

ing grants to increase basic cereal production. Yet it still cost the country at least twice as much to produce a tonne of maize as to import it.[13] The government thus adopted a broader food security strategy, focusing on access to food at affordable prices, irrespective of its source. This is an example that many other African countries ought to follow.

Third, most African countries are importing larger quantities of food from regional and global markets. Botswana's food imports have grown steadily over the last decade, reaching nearly P7 billion (USD0.8 billion) in 2007 (Figure 2). The country now imports approximately 90% of the national food supply.[14] The cereal balance sheet shows that for 2012/2013 the gross domestic requirement was 408,000 metric tonnes. However, the gross harvest was estimated at 31,000 tonnes and 494,000 tonnes were imported to ensure an adequate supply.[15] The importation of foodstuffs from neighbouring South Africa is partly a product of the growing presence and influence of supermarket chains in urban Botswana. This raises the question of whether a population that is increasingly dependent on supermarket supply chains is more or less vulnerable to food insecurity.

FIGURE 2: Total Value of Food Imports to Botswana (at 2007 Prices)

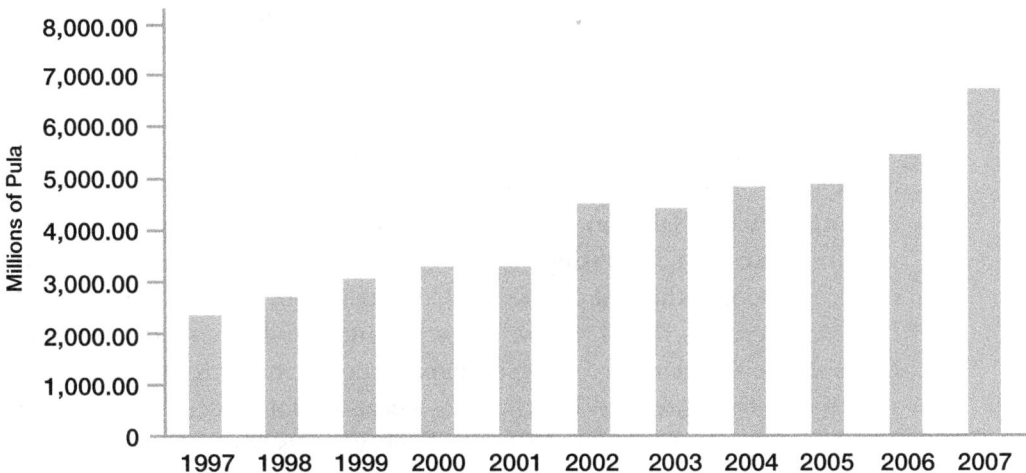

Source: BIDPA (2008)

2. THE GROWTH OF GABORONE

Gaborone, founded in 1963, is the capital and largest city in Botswana (Figure 3). It has grown dramatically from a population of 3,855 in 1964 to 231,626 in 2011 and is projected to reach about half a million per-

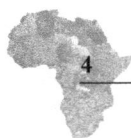

sons by 2021.[16] Gaborone has witnessed extensive public and private investment in the last decade, which has resulted in opportunities for wage employment and a modern lifestyle, with shopping malls, business districts, service industries and other facilities.[17] Its rapid growth stems largely from migration from rural areas where harsh agrarian conditions, recurrent drought and agricultural failure have caused people to depend increasingly on remittances for survival.[18]

Rapid urbanization in Gaborone has led to major urban sprawl and adjacent peripheral spaces have become integrated into the city region. The city covers over 170km². People in search of affordable accommodation and cheaper land have left the city centre in large numbers, resulting in a slow growth rate in the centre and the proliferation of peripheral settlements over a short space of time. Urban expansion has taken over farms that were in Broadhurst, Bonnington and Glen Valley and is encroaching on subsistence and commercial farmland in Kweneng and Kgatleng Districts, and Gaborone North.[19] These are areas where peri-urban agricultural enterprises in horticulture, piggery, poultry, rabbitry, small-stock rearing, dairying and broiler production are concentrated. Some farms have developed into huge townships. These include Pakalane Estates, Gaborone North and Mokolodi in the south, which are now well established. Urban expansion has also led to the appropriation of communal or tribal land and disenfranchisement of communal citizens.[20]

Gaborone's growth, which has outpaced the provision of housing, serviced urban land and supportive infrastructure, has generated a series of challenges.[21] High demand has increased the costs of urban development, making serviced land and houses difficult to afford. Urban standards require more formal housing solutions, which are often out of reach of the urban poor as the cost of materials, construction, land value and rental housing increases. Even where serviced land has been made available through the Accelerated Land Servicing Programme, it remains beyond the reach of its intended beneficiaries because plot prices and building material costs are not related to affordability assessments. Plot repossessions due to defaults on repayments have increased, further exacerbating the housing shortage. Low-income groups improvise accommodation by constructing unsafe housing in Old Naledi. Overcrowding exposes occupants of these small rooms to communicable diseases and stress, while lack of adequate water and sanitation facilities leaves them vulnerable to environmental ailments. All these developments have tended to work contrary to established development control codes and standards.

Rapid urbanization has been accompanied by rising levels of poverty. While the 2002/2003 Household Incomes and Expenditures Survey

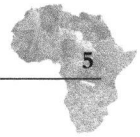

showed that urban was lower than rural poverty, the 2009/2010 Botswana Core Welfare Indicators Study found that urban poverty had increased.[22] Overall, the proportion of the national population living below the Poverty Datum Line (PDL) declined dramatically from 31% to 10%. At the same time, the proportion of urban residents below the PDL increased from 11% to 14%. Between 2002/2003 and 2009/2010, the proportion of households below the PDL dropped from 22% to 15%, while the proportion of urban households below the PDL increased from 9% to 13%.

A major concern with the rapid growth of the urban population is what has been described as "jobless growth" or the low labour absorptive capacity of Botswana's economy.[23] National unemployment is at 18%, much the same was it was in 2006.[24] However, the situation is more serious among youth, with 41% of 15–19-year-olds unemployed and 34% unemployment among 20–24-year-olds. Female rates of unemployment are higher in both age groups.

Given rising rates of inequality and poverty in urban Botswana, this AFSUN report examines whether and to what extent this is reflected in levels of food insecurity among the urban poor in Gaborone. The report is based on the results of a baseline survey conducted in 2008-2009 by researchers at the University of Botswana.

3. SURVEY METHODOLOGY

In an effort to improve the knowledge base about urban food security in Southern Africa, the African Food Security Urban Network (AFSUN) undertook a baseline study in 11 cities in nine countries in Southern Africa, including Gaborone. The survey data base contains information for 6,500 households and 28,700 individuals in the 11 cities. The survey was implemented in Gaborone in October 2008, with a sample of 400 households drawn from three of Gaborone's poorer areas: Old Naledi (150 households), White City/Bontleng (125 households) and Broadhurst (125 households) (Figure 3).

Old Naledi is a low-income "congested, overcrowded settlement" located south of the city adjacent to the north-south railway line.[25] The area started off as a squatter camp housing workers who had come to the city soon after independence to build the new capital. The initial plan was that once Gaborone was built the area would revert to its planned use as an industrial area, but this never happened. The migrants stayed put and were later joined by other migrants. The government has recently taken steps to improve the settlement by providing social, economic and line infrastructure, including schools, clinic, tarred/gravel roads, VIP latrines (now being replaced by a sewerage system), electricity, pumped water and street lights. The White City/Bontleng areas are immediately south of the city and south-west of the main Central Business District (CBD). Unlike Old Naledi, the two areas were planned as low- and medium-income areas with running water, tarred/gravel roads, and pit latrines giving way to a sewer system. Following upgrading, the areas have also received the excess population from Old Naledi. Most of the residents eke out a living in the informal sector. Broadhurst is located north of the city and has similar characteristics to Bontleng/White City with a mix of low- and some medium-income households.

FIGURE 3: Location of Survey Sites, Gaborone

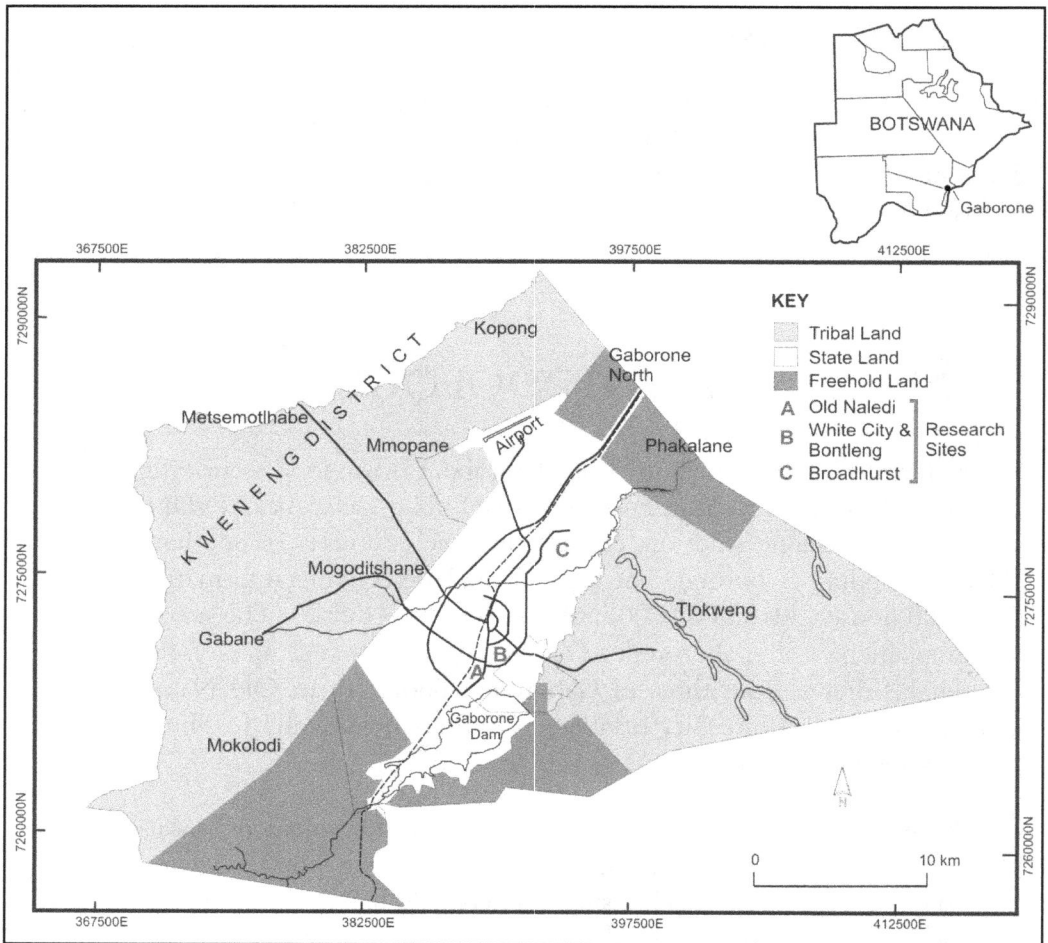

Source: Hovorka (2005)[26]

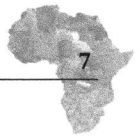

Systematic random sampling was used to select a sample of households in each site. The available maps of the city of Gaborone include clear layouts of streets and numbered households in the research sites. After the initial selection of a household on a street, the next two households were skipped and the fourth household was selected. Where there was no respondent in a selected household, the next household was selected for interview. At the household level, household heads or other responsible adults were selected to answer the questions on the survey.

The AFSUN survey used four international cross-cultural scales developed by the Food and Nutrition Technical Assistance Project (FANTA) to assess levels of food insecurity in Gaborone:

Household Food Insecurity Access Scale (HFIAS): The HFIAS measures the degree of food insecurity during the month prior to the survey.[27] An HFIAS score is calculated for each household based on answers to nine "frequency-of-occurrence" questions. The minimum score is 0 and the maximum is 27. The higher the score, the more food insecurity the household experienced.

Household Food Insecurity Access Prevalence (HFIAP) indicator: The HFIAP indicator uses the responses to the HFIAS questions to group households into four levels of household food insecurity: food secure, mildly food insecure, moderately food insecure and severely food insecure.

Household Dietary Diversity Scale (HDDS): Dietary diversity refers to how many food groups were consumed within the household in the previous 24 hours.[28] The maximum number, based on the FAO classification of food groups for Africa, is 12. An increase in the average number of different food groups consumed provides a quantifiable measure of improved household food access.

Months of Adequate Household Food Provisioning (MAHFP) indicator: The MAHFP indicator captures changes in the household's ability to ensure that food is available above a minimum level the year round.[29] Households are asked to identify in which months (during the past 12 months) they did not have access to sufficient food to meet their household needs.

4. HOUSEHOLD PROFILE

4.1 Demographic Characteristics

The average size of the surveyed households was only 3.0 (Table 2). The 2006 Botswana Demographic Survey found that the average size of Gaborone households was 3.3 (and the national average was 4.2).[30] In other words, poor urban households in Gaborone tend to be smaller than other urban and rural households. Second, the surveyed areas have a large proportion of female-centred households (47%) and male-centred households (23%) and smaller numbers of nuclear and extended family households.[31] The Demographic Survey found that 42% of Gaborone households were female-centred, which suggests that the poorer areas of the city have a slightly greater proportion of female-centred households.[32] Third, only 25% of surveyed household heads were married or cohabiting. This is relatively close to the proportion of nuclear and extended family households (at 28%) and suggests that most of the heads of male- and female-centred households are single. The low rates of marriage are consistent with broader trends in Botswana: marriage rates have been steadily declining in recent decades and only 31% of all household heads in the country were married in 2001.[33]

The total population of the sampled households was relatively young, with 23% under the age of 15 and 64% under the age of 30. The latter figure is not dissimilar to the regional average of 68%. However, there is a marked difference in the proportion of household members under the age of 15 (23% versus 32%). This may partly reflect the practice in Botswana of parents working in the urban areas and leaving their children in the care of grandparents and other relatives in the rural areas. However, the number of children in the sample was still relatively high. There were very few adopted children or orphans despite the fact that the number of AIDS orphans is estimated by some to be as high as 100,000 in Botswana.

Consistent with the growth of urban areas in Botswana, the survey found that the majority of the residents of the surveyed areas were migrants. Only 28% of the household members were born in urban areas (23% in Gaborone itself and 5% in another urban area). In total, then, more than two-thirds (69%) of the surveyed population were born outside the city and had subsequently moved to Gaborone. The 2006 Botswana Demographic Survey found that 40% of the national population had migrated at least once.[34] This is considerably lower than the Gaborone figure, probably because it includes a large number of children and youth who are still living where they were born. Of all 11 cities in the AFSUN survey, Gaborone had the highest number of migrant households (that is, households in which every member was born outside the city) at 67% and the lowest number of non-migrant households (5%) (Table 3).

TABLE 2: Demographic Characteristics of Households	
Household characteristics	
Household size	No. of members
Average	3.0
Median	3.0
Smallest	1.0
Largest	10.0
Household structure	%
Female-centred	47
Male-centred	23
Nuclear	20
Extended	8
Individual characteristics	
Sex	%
Male	43
Female	57
Age	%
0–15	23
16–29	41
30–44	24
45+	12
Marital status (>=15 years)	%
Unmarried	71
Married	11
Living together/cohabiting	14
Divorced	0
Widowed	3
Relationship to household head	%
Spouse/partner	16
Son/daughter	52
Parent	<1
Adopted child/orphan	<1
Other relative	18
Non-relative	14

TABLE 3: Proportion of Migrant and Non-Migrant Households

City	Migrant households (% of total)	Mixed households (% of total)	Non-migrant households (% of total)
Gaborone	67	28	5
Cape Town, South Africa	54	40	6
Msunduzi, South Africa	48	43	9
Windhoek, Namibia	49	40	11
Johannesburg, South Africa	42	35	23
Maseru, Lesotho	37	52	11
Manzini, Swaziland	32	55	13
Lusaka, Zambia	24	56	20
Blantyre, Malawi	17	65	18
Maputo, Mozambique	11	78	11
Harare, Zimbabwe	9	78	13
Total	38	49	13

4.2 Economic Characteristics

The educational levels of the sampled population were generally low (Table 4). For example, 61% of adult household members only had a primary school education or lower. Another 12% had completed high school and 9% had a post-secondary qualification. The generally low educational attainment of the population would tend to confine them to lower-skilled, lower-paying jobs or to unemployment. The survey found that 62% of adults in the poorer areas of Gaborone were unemployed (Table 5). Of these, 15% were actively looking for work and 47% were not. Among the sample, 26% were in full-time employment and 11% were employed part-time. These figures contrast sharply with national figures, which show that in 2006 the unemployment level was 31% (with 14% looking and 17% not looking).[35] National rates of unemployment were 34% among women and 25% among men in 2006. In the survey areas, 57% of men and 68% of women were unemployed. The majority of the unemployed, both men and women, were not actively looking for work.

At the national level, there is a clear occupational division by gender, with men dominant in mining, construction, transportation and, to a lesser extent, the civil service. Women dominate wholesale and retail, tourism, education and domestic work.[36] The less-educated workforce in Gaborone's poorer areas tends to work in lower-skilled, low-income sectors (Table 6). Among the 20% of skilled white-collar workers in the survey areas there were similar numbers of women and men. However, within the blue-collar occupations, men predominate in skilled manual labour (primarily construction) and women in domestic work. More women than men also work in the informal economy.

TABLE 4 : Highest Level of Education	Male (%)	Female (%)	Total (%)
No formal schooling	7	10	9
Some primary school	12	12	12
Primary completed	42	42	42
Some high school	8	10	9
High school completed	14	12	12
Post-secondary (non-university)	8	5	6
Some university	6	6	6
University completed	3	3	3
N	332	465	797

TABLE 5: Employment Status	Male (%)	Female (%)	Total (%)
Working full-time	32	21	26
Working part-time/casual	12	10	11
Not working – looking	13	19	15
Not working – not looking	44	50	47

TABLE 6: Occupations of Employed Household Members	Male (%)	Female (%)	Total (%)
Skilled/white collar	18	20	18
Managerial office worker	2	2	2
Professionals	9	10	9
Office worker/civil servant	6	7	6
Employer/manager	1	1	1
Semi-skilled/blue collar	46	34	40
Skilled manual worker	13	4	9
Service worker	11	10	11
Security	8	2	5
Truck driver	5	<1	3
Supervisor ("foreman")	2	<1	1
Police/military	2	<1	1
Miner	2	<1	1
Domestic worker	2	18	9
Other	14	32	22
Self-employed entrepreneur	9	15	12
Informal economy	5	17	10

Just over half of the surveyed households (51%) receive income from wage work and 24% from casual work (Table 6). Other minor sources of income include rent (10%), informal business (8%), formal business (8%) and social grants (6%). Remittances (from household members working on Botswana's diamond mines) are received by 8% of households. The proportion of households that receive income from the sale of urban farm products is a mere 0.3%.

When this data is disaggregated by household type, various differences emerge. The most important from a food security perspective is that 80% of nuclear households earn wage income compared with 56% of male-centred households and only 43% of female-centred households (Table 7). More nuclear households are also involved in formal and informal businesses, usually run by the female spouse or partner (28% versus 16% of female-centred households). As a result, nuclear households have the highest average incomes (at P2,813 per month), followed by extended family households (P2,733 per month) and male-centred households (P2,403 per month). Female-centred households earn considerably less on average than the other types of household (P1,674 per month) and are therefore far more vulnerable to food insecurity.

TABLE 7: Sources of Income by Household Type					
	All (% of households)	Female-centred (% of households)	Male-centred (% of households)	Nuclear (% of households)	Extended (% of households)
Wage work	51	43	56	80	45
Casual work	24	25	22	24	15
Rent	10	9	8	13	15
Formal business	8	9	6	9	12
Informal business	8	7	7	15	3
Remittances	8	10	7	4	15
Social grants	6	8	2	3	6
Gifts	5	8	6	1	3
Aid	2	4	2	1	9
Urban agriculture	<1	<1	0	0	0
N	379	188	90	78	33
Average monthly income		P1,674	P2,403	P2,813	P2,733

5. LEVELS OF FOOD INSECURITY

Levels of food security in Gaborone proved to be marginally better than in several other cities surveyed (including Manzini, Harare, Maseru,

Lusaka and Msunduzi), although many households reported difficulties in meeting their food needs. The mean HFIAS score for Gaborone was 10.8, comparable to the poorer areas of Cape Town but higher (indicating greater levels of food insecurity) than cities such as Maputo, Windhoek, Blantyre and Johannesburg (Table 8).

TABLE 8: Gaborone HFIAS Scores Compared to Other Cities

	Mean HFIAS	Median HFIAS	No.
Manzini, Swaziland	14.9	14.7	489
Harare, Zimbabwe	14.7	16.0	454
Maseru, Lesotho	12.8	13.0	795
Lusaka, Zambia	11.5	11.0	386
Msunduzi, South Africa	11.3	11.0	548
Gaborone, Botswana	10.8	11.0	391
Cape Town, South Africa	10.7	11.0	1,026
Maputo, Mozambique	10.4	10.0	389
Windhoek, Namibia	9.3	9.0	436
Blantyre, Malawi	5.3	3.7	431
Johannesburg, South Africa	4.7	1.5	976

The Household Food Insecurity Access Prevalence (HFIAP) indicator divides the households into four groups: food secure (12% of the total), mildly food insecure (7%), moderately food insecure (19%) and severely food insecure (62%) (Table 9). Food insecurity therefore appears to be endemic in the poorer parts of Gaborone. Botswana's "economic miracle" is clearly not reaching many of these households.

TABLE 9: Levels of Food Insecurity by Type of Household

	Female-centred (%)	Male-centred (%)	Nuclear (%)	Extended (%)	Total (%)
Food secure	13	12	13	3	12
Mildly food insecure	4	4	15	7	7
Moderately food insecure	13	22	15	24	19
Severely food insecure	64	61	57	66	62

In terms of the relationship between household structure and food security, some important differences can be identified. Female-centred households do not appear to be significantly more food insecure than other types of household, as they are in many other SADC cities.[37] Given the lower rates of participation in the formal economy, the relegation of many women to the lower end of the labour market and the fact that the

average incomes of these households are well-below those of other types of household, this is a surprising finding. Nearly two-thirds of female-centred households are severely food insecure but so are 66% of extended family households, 61% of male-centred households and 57% of nuclear households. In addition, there are not significantly fewer food-secure female-centred households.

There are two possible explanations for this: first, the food-secure female-centred households could be headed by white-collar workers with a regular wage. For example, the maximum household income among the female-centred household group was P12,050 per month, which is more than five times the average. A second explanation is that women heads of households prioritize food expenditures and therefore spend a greater proportion of their income on food. There is some evidence from the survey to support this proposition. For example, in female-centred households, 39% of total household expenditure is on food, compared with 32% in male-centred households and 27% in extended households. In nuclear households, where women have some control over the household budget, food expenditures are also higher (at 34%) but not as high as in female-centred households. Extended family households are the most food insecure despite the fact that they have much higher household income than female-centred households. This may be because these households tend to be larger and have more mouths to feed.

Several recent studies of nutrition and dietary diversity among the elderly and youth in urban and rural settings in Botswana show a recurrent pattern of poor dietary diversity among the most vulnerable groups in society.[38] Specific studies of groups of urban poor in Gaborone confirm that dietary diversity is extremely low with negative nutritional outcomes. For example, one study of 522 young children in Gaborone found that 11% were stunted and 14% were wasted. Stunting and wasting ranged from 9% and 4% in middle- and high-income neighbourhoods to 18% and 21% in low-income neighbourhoods respectively.[39]

The FANTA Household Dietary Diversity Score captures the foods consumed in the household in the 24 hours before the survey and groups them into 12 food groups. The higher the score, the more diverse the diet. The median HDDS score for the Gaborone households was 7 out of 12 (mean of 6.5). These numbers indicate relatively low dietary diversity, although it is notable that households in Gaborone do enjoy a more diverse diet than the regional norm. For example, 48% of households in the regional sample had a score of 5 or lower compared with only 32% of the Gaborone households (Table 10). A greater proportion of Gaborone households also scored 7 or more (37% compared with 27% of the regional sample), another indicator of a more diverse diet. Also important in assessing the quality of the diet are the food groups consumed (Figure 4). The majority of households had consumed cereals (97%), sugars (74%), oils/fats (63%) and "others" such as tea and coffee (76%). There was also relatively high consumption of meat and vegetables, which can be attributed to the traditional Batswana staple meal of maize meal, vegetable relish and beef.

TABLE 10: Household Dietary Diversity		
HDD score	Gaborone (cumulative %)	Regional (cumulative %)
1	5	2
2	10	13
3	16	23
4	23	34
5	32	48
6	43	61
7	63	73
8	78	83
9	88	90
10	92	94
11	95	96
12	100	100

FIGURE 4: Types of Food Eaten in Previous 24 Hours

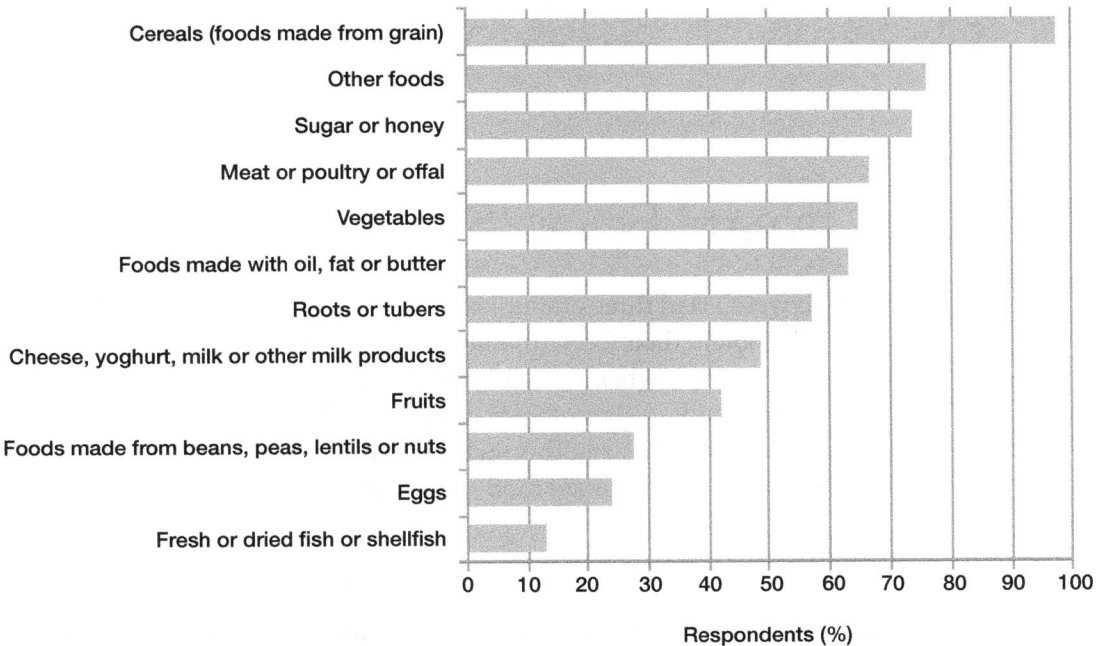

Respondents (%)

The Months of Adequate Household Food Provisioning (MAHFP) score for Gaborone was 9. Some 60% of households had experienced a period of inadequate food provisioning in the previous 12 months. Figure 5 shows the variation in levels of food security of all households combined during the previous year. Interestingly, the peaks and troughs do not correlate with the agricultural cycle, with the rainy season from November to March and the dry season from April to October. This would be consistent with a population that relies more on food imports than local production. The fluctuations are associated with spending cycles, most notably the jump in food shortage in January following December festivities. The jump in September is probably associated with preparations for Botswana Day festivities.

FIGURE 5: Months of Food Shortage

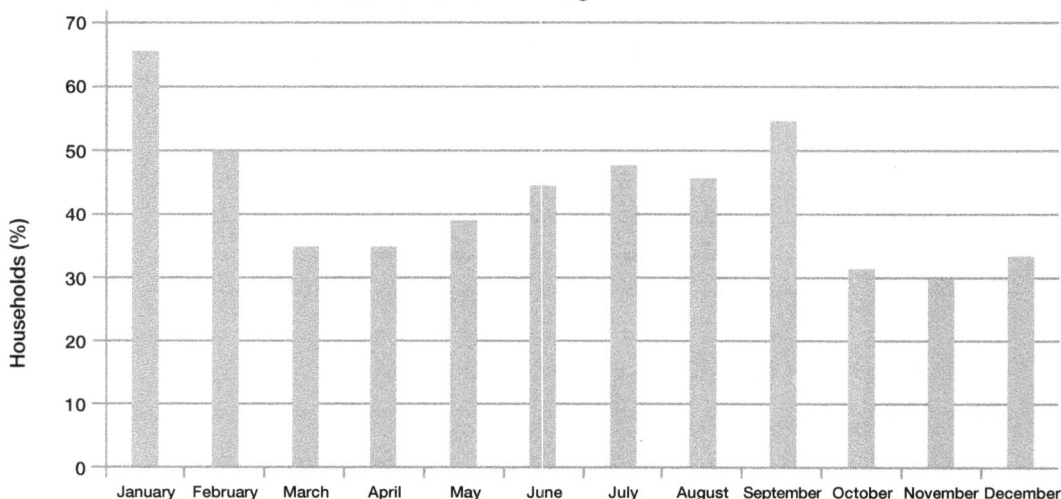

6. Urban Food Sources

Households were asked three questions about their food sources: (a) where they normally obtain their food; (b) how frequently they obtain food from these sources; and (c) where they obtained food in the previous week. In the case of (a) and (c), households could identify more than one food source. In presenting the data, this section therefore looks at the proportion of households that obtained food from each of the possible sources.

6.1 Supermarkets

Botswana's proximity to South Africa has meant that it is increasingly integrated into the supermarket-driven food supply chains that dominate that country's food retail sector. Southern Africa's "supermarket revolution" has transformed the way in which urban (and rural) residents of Botswana source their food.[40] Supermarkets have expanded in Botswana over the past 30 years, a growth driven by a rapidly increasing urban population, a growing middle-class and a favourable economic and political climate for investment including trade liberalization and stable democracy.[41] Supermarkets handle around 50-60% of food retail in cities and major urban villages in Botswana. Within Gaborone, supermarkets are scattered around the city and are accessible to most urban consumers (Figure 6).

FIGURE 6: Location of Supermarkets in Gaborone

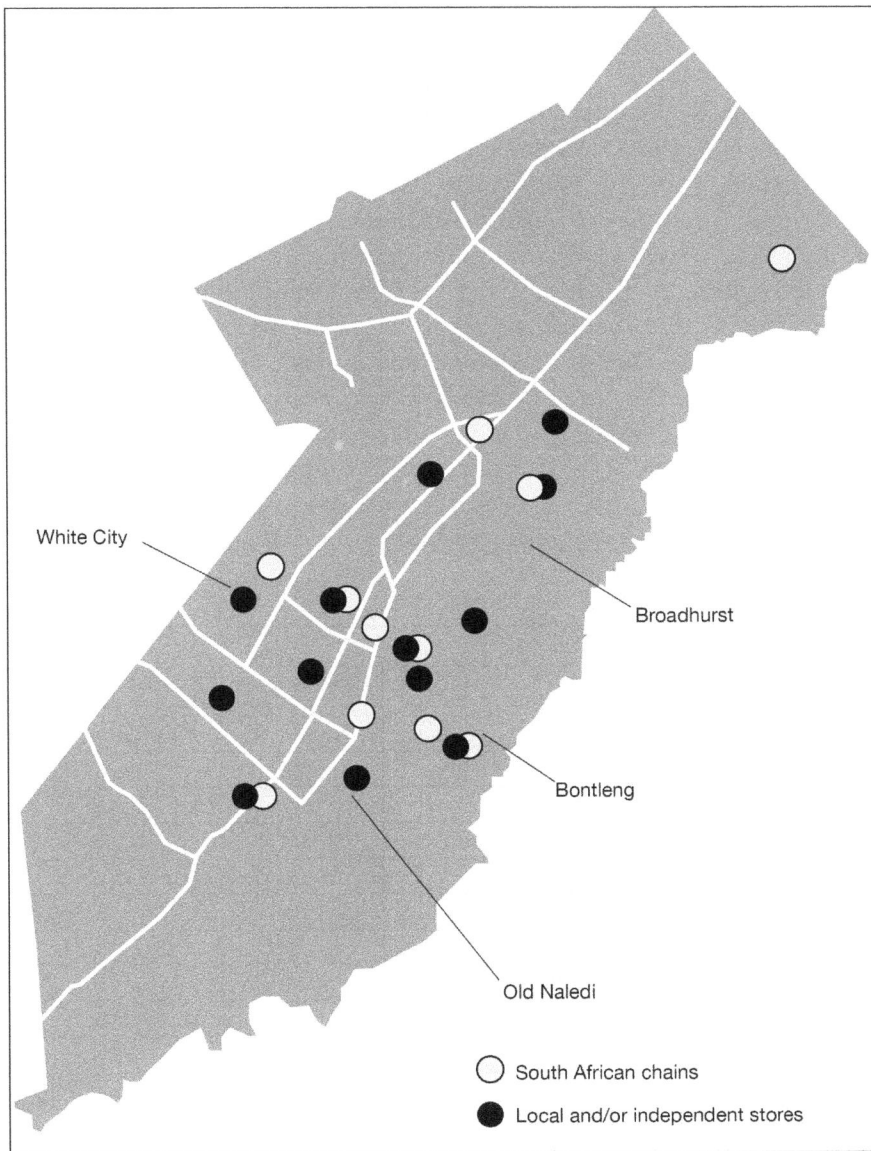

There are two main types of supermarkets. First, there are the major South African supermarket chains (such as Shoprite, Spar and Woolworths) that have become increasingly well-established in Gaborone's urban food market. Second, there are smaller, locally-owned supermarkets that tend to target poorer areas of the city. Some Gaborone-based supermarket chains have been expanding to towns outside the capital. In a recent reversal of the trend of supermarket expansion from South Africa to other African countries, one of these chains (Choppies) has been opening stores in South Africa.[42]

Supermarkets sell a variety of perishable and non-perishable products, including maize meal, sugar, flour and milk, at significantly lower costs than most other food outlets within Gaborone.[43] Low-income households take advantage of the central role that supermarkets play in the food system, using them to purchase staple foods in bulk.[44] It is also worth noting that supermarkets have increased the availability of highly-processed foods, which poses dietary concerns especially given growing evidence of a nutrition transition and the co-existence of diet-related disease and obesity.[45] The survey found that supermarkets are easily the most important food source for the urban poor in Gaborone (Table 11), with 92% of households using them as a normal food source. As many as 73% of households had also purchased food at supermarkets in the week prior to the survey. A third of the households said they buy from supermarkets at least once a week (Table 12). Another two-thirds shop there at least once a month. Only 4% of households never shop at supermarkets. Supermarkets are a more important food source in Gaborone than in any other city in the AFSUN survey, including the three South African cities.[46]

TABLE 11: Sources of Food		
	Normal source (% of households)	In previous week (% of households)
Supermarkets	92	73
Small outlets	54	52
Informal food economy	29	23
Urban agriculture	5	2
Food aid	5	5
Food remittances	4	4
Sharing meals with neighbours/other households	21	16
Food from neighbours/other households	21	18
Borrow food from others	4	3

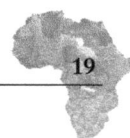

TABLE 12: Frequency of Usage of Food Sources						
	At least 5 days a week (%)	At least once a week (%)	At least once a month (%)	At least once every 6 months (%)	Less than once a year (%)	Never (%)
Supermarkets	10	20	65	1	0	4
Small outlets	20	20	15	2	0	43
Informal food economy	13	11	4	1	0	71
Urban agriculture	0	1	1	2	1	95
Food aid	6	0	0	0	0	94
Food remittances	0	0	2	2	0	96
Sharing meals with neighbours/other households	4	9	7	1	1	78
Food from neighbours/ other households	3	9	8	1	0	79
Borrow food from others	2	1	0	0	0	97

6.2 Informal and Small Retail Food Economy

According to the Central Statistics Office, Botswana's informal economy has been expanding "very fast" in recent years.[47] The CSO's 2007 Informal Sector Survey estimated the total number of informal enterprises at 44,000 of which 28,000 were owned by women. The number of enterprises had increased by 54% since the 1999 Informal Sector Survey. Gaborone had a larger share of the enterprises than any other part of the country (around 11,000 or 23% of the total). On the other hand, another study has suggested that the presence of South African supermarkets and the absence of a supportive policy environment means that the informal economy in Botswana is neither large nor flourishing.[48] This might suggest that the informal food economy in Gaborone is not a major source of food for the urban poor. The AFSUN survey confirmed that the informal food economy is relatively unimportant for the majority of poor urban households. Only 29% of the households said they normally obtain food from informal sources and just 23% had done so in the previous week. Most of this is consumption of cooked street food during the day. As many as 71% of the households never obtain food from informal sources.

No other city in the AFSUN survey has such a relatively insignificant informal food economy. In the region as a whole, 70% of households normally obtain food from the informal economy and in some cities (such as Blantyre, Maputo, Lusaka and Harare) the proportion is over 90%.. Small retail outlets are also far less important in Gaborone than in most other cities. Around half the households obtain food from this source on a regular basis, compared with a regional average of 68%. As many as 43% of Gaborone households never obtain food from small outlets.

6.3 Urban Agriculture

The Botswana Ministry of Agriculture encourages urban and peri-urban agriculture initiatives as a policy strategy for ensuring urban food security in an era of rapid urbanization, economic decline, urban poverty and HIV and AIDS.[49] Empirical studies from Gaborone have highlighted the challenging environmental conditions that limit agricultural production, with urban and peri-urban agriculture offering limited prospects for the urban poor.[50] On the other hand, well-educated middle-income entrepreneurs involved mainly in poultry farming do generate foodstuffs for the urban market.[51] These entrepreneurs are adept at taking advantage of government funding schemes and land tenure policy in Gaborone, creating productive agricultural ventures.[52] The potential for urban agriculture to address food insecurity tends to be overemphasized, given its limited share in income and overall agricultural production.[53] The insignificance of urban agriculture as an income source for Gaborone's urban poor is demonstrated in Table 7 above. Urban agriculture is also unimportant as a household food source for the urban poor. Only 4% of households consume some home-grown produce during the course of a year and 97% never do so (Table 12).

6.4 Rural–Urban Transfers

A 2003 study of 360 households in the Broadhurst area of Gaborone found that the vast majority of households had close rural links.[54] Of the household heads, 82% were involved in some form of rural activity, including cattle rearing, keeping small stock, poultry farming and arable agriculture. As many as 65% of the household heads owned farmland/fields in rural areas, 64% owned livestock and 57% owned cattle posts/grazing fields. Links were maintained through two-way visits, remittances to rural family members, and the exchange of goods. The study found that the transfer of goods, including agricultural produce, was relatively unimportant with only 9% of households receiving goods from rural areas.[55]

The AFSUN survey confirmed that rural-urban food transfers are not a particularly significant phenomenon, and certainly nowhere near as important as in cities such as Windhoek, Harare and Lusaka (Table 13).[56] Three-quarters of the households never receive food transfers from outside Gaborone. However, food transfers certainly do assist a minority of households to deal with the challenge of food insecurity. A total of 16%

of households regularly receive transfers from rural areas, 4% receive food from other urban centres and 3% receive food from both. Nuclear households tend to have the strongest links in terms of rural–urban transfers (29%) and female–centred households the weakest (16%). The most common types of food transferred are peas, beans and nuts, cereals and vegetables.

TABLE 13: Informal Food Transfers to Gaborone				
	Female-centred (%)	Male-centred (%)	Nuclear (%)	Extended (%)	Total (%)
Rural areas only	13	11	28	21	16
Urban areas only	4	3	4	3	4
Both areas	3	7	1	3	3
No transfers	80	78	63	73	76

6.5 Other Sources

A minority of households rely on other households to meet some of their food needs. For example, 21% said they share meals with, or receive food from, neighbours and/or relatives. Just over 15% had done so in the week prior to the survey. However, nearly 80% of households never obtain food this way. Food borrowing is much less important (with only 4% sometimes borrowing from others). Small numbers of households (4-5%) receive regular food aid and food remittances.

7. FOOD INSECURITY AND HIGH FOOD PRICES

A 2008 BIDPA study of rising food prices in Botswana showed that the cost of a basket of basic foodstuffs had risen from P332 to P381 between 2006 and May 2008 (in 2008 prices), a real increase of 15%.[57] Bread flour, maize meal, meat and milk showed the greatest proportional increases, while the cost of vegetables, sorghum, sugar and salt remained relatively stable. Prices for most products continued to rise steeply during the remainder of 2008 and into 2009. Given the reliance of poor households in Gaborone on food purchase and food imports, these urban dwellers are likely to be particularly vulnerable to rapid food price increases, but the government seemed to focus its concern about food price inflation on rural residents.

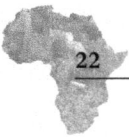

A high proportion of survey respondents noted that their economic conditions had deteriorated in the year prior to the survey (25% much worse, 18% worse). Only a few (18%) noted that their conditions had got better or much better in the past year. Only 17% of households said they had never had to go without food in the previous six months because it was unaffordable (Table 14). Extended family households (the most food-insecure type overall) had the lowest incidence of never going without (6%). At the other end of the spectrum, more nuclear households than any other type went without on a daily basis. The majority of all types of household went without on a weekly or monthly basis (52%), which correlates with the period prior to their weekly or monthly shop at the local supermarket.

TABLE 14: Frequency of Going Without Food in Previous Six Months Due to Price Increases

	Female-centred (%)	Male-centred (%)	Nuclear (%)	Extended (%)	Total (%)
Every day	16	18	25	12	18
At least once a week	30	30	22	30	28
Once a month	23	25	25	27	24
Never	17	18	20	6	17

8. CONCLUSIONS AND RECOMMENDATIONS

The AFSUN survey results show that not everyone is benefitting from Botswana's strong and growing economy and that many of the urban poor in Gaborone experience extremely high levels of food insecurity. The survey collected data on a broad range of issues that affect household food insecurity and illustrates how in Gaborone, a relatively wealthy city, a high number of households are food insecure. Approximately four out of five households in the survey reported severe or moderate food insecurity. In contrast, only 18% were either food secure or mildly food insecure. Income level is a particularly important determinant of food insecurity as most households access food from the marketplace rather than grow their own. The data show a significant correlation between household income and food security, with the poorest households being most severely affected by food insecurity.

The pace of urbanization in Botswana is unlikely to decline, particularly in view of the country's post-independence history of temporary and semi-permanent movement off the land and given the continued expansion of the formal-sector economy. Barring the imposition of artificial controls on movement, which is extremely unlikely to happen, people will continue to migrate to towns in increasing numbers. There is an argument that to slow down migration the government should accelerate the provision of services and make the rural areas more attractive through rural development. While this might alleviate hardship in the countryside, it is highly unlikely to stop Botswana's urban transition. The Botswana government and the Gaborone City Council are under serious pressure to handle the implications of rapid urbanization with respect to service provision, housing, transportation, health care, education, employment and the impact of HIV and AIDS. What this report shows is that food insecurity is an equally serious challenge requiring urgent attention.

The short- and long-term impacts of chronic food insecurity on Gaborone's population are likely to be considerable unless this problem is urgently addressed. The problem is in some sense invisible because there appears to be no shortage of food in the shops and on the streets of this booming city. The challenge is not one of food supply but food accessibility and food quality. The default food security policy strategy in most African countries is usually directed at increasing smallholder agricultural production. Despite official preoccupation with low agricultural production within Botswana, the country is highly dependent on the supply of foods from neighbouring South Africa. The advanced agricultural production and marketing system in South Africa ensures that South African-owned and local supermarkets in Botswana are generously supplied with a variety of products all year round. This has its positive elements, as Batswana do not need to worry about seasonality and crop failure.

There are some government efforts to improve access to local (Botswana) fresh produce, for example, the establishment of Botswana Horticultural Market in the Broadhurst Industrial area in Gaborone in 2008.[58] This commission-based market, where market agents sell fresh foods to buyers and wholesalers on behalf of famers, has a capacity of about 3,600 tonnes and cold storage of about 320 tonnes. The market has been able to attract local producers from several parts of the country including Kasane, Tuli Block, Bobonong, Mahalapye, Gaborone Talana farms and Barolong farms, although its clientele still largely consists of retailers and wholesalers rather than individuals. It has been suggested that for greater efficiency it would be important to reduce the number of staff, allow cash transactions on small food quantities as transactions are currently via computerized smart cards, and allow farmers direct contact with buyers.[59]

On the other hand, the availability of food for purchase discourages a greater uptake of urban agriculture to supplement incomes, food supplies and provide better nutrition. There are vast areas in the city where this activity could be carried out, including on road verges, along infrastructure rights of way, rivers and stream valleys that are unsuitable to build on and many other open spaces in the city. Both permanent and temporary crops could be grown here to help feed the city's population. However, such urban agriculture as exists in Gaborone tends to be undertaken by middle-class households that are able to earn income from these activities. The urban poor might follow suit if there is a chance that effort invested in urban agriculture would lead to increased household income. There is much less chance that they will do so simply to grow food for home consumption.

Around Gaborone, all neighbourhoods (both high and low income), are well serviced with food access points. Malls have become a defining characteristic of the city and most include several supermarkets. Complementing the supermarkets are general provision stores (cash and carry), stores at filling stations, fast-food chains, restaurants and street vendors. While sufficient food is available at these diverse access points, the major issue is affordability and, more specifically, affordability of nutritious foods. The profit-making and pricing strategies of these South African retail outlets need much closer examination and even regulation, particularly during times of food price escalation. Corporate social responsibility should also be encouraged to minimize food wastage, support feeding programmes and foster entrepreneurship.

Poor urban households in Gaborone depend heavily on wage income as a survival strategy. The few households with a member in decent paid employment are significantly less food insecure than the rest. A number of households do have members in low-wage or casual work and this does not insulate them from food insecurity. Poor households do not have a lot of other income-generating possibilities. A small number receive remittances from relatives working elsewhere and a few participate in the informal economy. But, by and large, the informal economy is relatively small for a city the size of Gaborone and with such high rates of unemployment. It is clear that Botswana's economic trajectory, for all its positive dimensions, is not leading to inclusive growth.

The informal economy is a permanent fixture and should be accorded due attention and support. Entrepreneurial initiatives could be much better nurtured, rather than being hamstrung by numerous zoning and licensing regulations. If allowed to develop freely, the informal sector, which can be particularly important for the poorest sectors of society, will evolve in

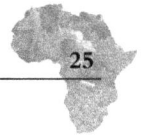

response to need. Price and accessibility of goods and services will reflect a balanced relationship between supply and demand, and thus be within the reach of a greater proportion of the population. This in turn generates capital and at the same time is a convenience for those customers with least mobility. Furthermore, in Botswana, where there is little tradition of entrepreneurship, the informal sector is an important component of future commercial and industrial development.

In terms of local dietary knowledge and skills, there is growing concern about the effects of urbanization, with its concomitant supermarket expansion and lifestyle change, on the people of Botswana. For example, urban adolescents in Botswana are at growing risk of obesity given their high consumption of snacks and fizzy drinks coupled with low consumption of healthy foods including fruits and traditional meals.[60] Traditional diets in Botswana include maize or sorghum with meat and vegetable relish or samp and beans, which provide a relatively balanced meal. However, there is an increased tendency for maize meal to be mixed with processed packaged soups in low-income households in Gaborone. The survey results also show a low proportion of households eating foods made of beans, lentils and peas, which are healthy protein sources. Economic and lifestyle considerations that come with living in the city trump traditional knowledge around proper dietary habits.

ENDNOTES

1   International Monetary Fund (IMF), "Botswana" IMF Country Report No. 12/235, Washington DC, 2012, p. 4.

2   O. Selolwane, ed, *Poverty Reduction and Changing Policy Regimes in Botswana* (London: Palgrave Macmillan, 2012).

3   CSO, "2005/6 Labour Force Report" Central Statistics Office, Gaborone, 2008.

4   IMF, "Botswana" p. 6.

5   Ibid., p. 5.

6   P. Moepeng, "The Role of Macroeconomic Policy Towards Food Security in Botswana" Report for Botswana Institute of Development Policy Analysis (BIDPA), Gaborone, 2003.

7   C. Stevens, "Food Aid and Nutrition: The Case of Botswana" *Food Policy* 3 (1978):18-28; J. Cathie and H. Dick, *Food Security and Macroeconomic Stabilization: A Case Study of Botswana, 1965-1984* (Tuebingen: Mohr, 1987); J. Cathie and R. Hermann, "The Southern African Customs Union, Cereal Price Policy in South Africa, and Food Security in Botswana" *Journal of Development Studies* 24 (1988): 394-414; S. Asefa, "Managing Food Security Action Programs in Botswana" International Development Papers No. 36, Department of Agricultural, Food, and Resource Economics, Michigan State University, 1989; J. Hesselberg, "Food

security in Botswana" *Norsk Geografisk Tidsskrift* 47 (1993): 183-95; K. Belbase and R. Morgan, "Food Security and Nutrition Monitoring for Drought Relief Management: The Case of Botswana" *Food Policy* 19 (1994): 285-300; T. Fako and L. Molamu, "The Seven-Year Drought, Household Food Security and Vulnerable Groups in Botswana" *Pula: Botswana Journal of African Studies* 9(1995); I. Mazonde, "Social Transformation and Food Security in the Household: The Experience of Rural Botswana" In F. Krueger, G. Rakelmann and P. Schierholz, eds., *Botswana* (Hamburg: LIT Verlag, 2000), pp.53-74; C. Lado, "Environmental and Socio-Economic Factors Behind Food Security Policy Strategies in Botswana" *Development Southern Africa* 18 (2001): 141-68. P. Moepeng, "The Role of Macroeconomic Policy Towards Food Security in Botswana" Working Paper, Botswana Institute for Development Policy Analysis (BIDPA), Gaborone, 2003; G. Legwaila, W. Mojeremane, M. Madisa, R. Mmolotsi and M. Rampart, "Potential of Traditional Food Plants in Rural Household Food Security in Botswana" *Journal of Horticulture and Forestry* 3 (2011): 171–7; L. Neudeck, L. Avelino, P. Bareetseng, B.Ngwenya, D.Teketay and M. Motsholapheko, "The Contribution of Edible Wild Plants to Food Security, Dietary Diversity and Income of Households in Shorobe Village, Northern Botswana" *Ethnobotany Research & Applications* 10 (2012).

8   K. Sebolaaphuti, "The Effect of HIV/AIDS on Household Food Security: A Case Study of Bokaa, a Rural Area in Botswana" MA Thesis, University of Stellenbosch, 2005; K. Kobotswang, "The Impact of HIV and AIDS on Food Security and Agricultural Production in Botswana" Working Document, Food, Agriculture and Natural Resources Policy Analysis Network (FANRPAN), Pretoria, 2006; B. Ngwenya and K. Mosepele, "HIV/AIDS, Artisanal Fishing and Food Security in the Okavango Delta, Botswana" *Physics and Chemistry of the Earth, Parts A/B/C* 32 (2007): 1339-49; J. Moreki, R. Dikeme and B. Poroga, "The Role of Village Poultry in Food Security and HIV/AIDS Mitigation in Chobe District of Botswana" *Livestock Research for Rural Development* 22 (2010); R. Hitchcock and W. Babchuk, "Food, Health, Development, and HIV/AIDS in a Remote Area of Southern Africa" *Annals of Anthropological Practice* 35 (2011): 204-18; J. Moreki, "Family Chickens, Poverty Alleviation, Food Security and HIV/AIDS Mitigation: The Case of BONEPWA+" *Journal of AIDS and HIV Research* 4 (2012): 229-33.

9   N-B Kandala, E. Campbell, S. Rakgoasi, B. Madi-Segwagwe and T. Fako, "The Geography of HIV/AIDS Prevalence Rates in Botswana" *HIV/AIDS – Research and Palliative Care* 4 (2012): 95-102.

10   H. Wittman, "Food Sovereignty: A New Rights Framework for Food and Nature?" *Environment and Society: Advances in Research* 2 (2011): 87-105.

11   P. Zhou, T. Simbini, G. Ramokgotlwane, S. Hachigonta, L. Sibanda and T. Thomas, "Southern African Agriculture and Climate Change: Botswana" International Food Policy Research Institute, Washington DC, 2012; M. Williams, "Contextualizing Youth Entrepreneurship: The Case of Botswana and the Young Farmers Fund (YFF)" MA Thesis, University of Guelph, 2012.

12   Government of Botswana, "National Agricultural Policy:1991" at http://www.moa.gov.bw/?nav=agricpolicy

13   C. Lado, "Environmental and Socio-Economic Factors Behind Food Security Policy Strategies in Botswana" *Development Southern Africa* 18 (2001): 141-68.

14   W. Moseley, "A Glimpse of Africa's Future? Botswana's Conundrum of

Spectacular Growth with Hunger" at http://world.edu/a-glimpse-of-africas-future-botswanas-conundrum-of-spectacular-growth-with-hunger/; P. Kebakile, "Rising Global Food Prices : Causes and Implications for Botswana" Briefing Paper, Botswana Institute for Development Policy Analysis (BIDPA), Gaborone, 2008.

15   FANR, "SADC Food Security Update" at http://www.sadc.int/fanr/aims/rews/SADC_Food_Security_Update_-_August_14_2012.pdf

16   Central Statistics Office, *2011 Botswana Population and Housing Census: Population of Towns, Villages and Associated Localities*, Gaborone, 2012.

17   B. Cavric and M. Kelner. "Managing Development of a Rapidly Growing African City: A Case of Gaborone, Botswana." *Geoadria* 11(2006): 93-121; M. Ritsema, "Gaborone is Growing like a Baby: Life Expectancies and Death Expectations in Urban Botswana" *Africa Development* 33(2010); T. Gwebu, "Botswana's Mining Path to Urbanisation and Poverty Alleviation" *Journal of Contemporary African Studies* 30 (2012): 611-30.

18   E. Campbell, "Moderating Poverty: The Role of Remittances from Migration in Botswana" *Africa Development* 33 (2008): 91-115; E. Campbell, "The Role of Remittances in Botswana: Does Internal Migration Really Reward Sending Families?" *Population, Space and Place* 16 (2010): 152-64; E. Campbell and N-B. Kandala, "Remittances from Internal Migration and Poverty in Botswana" *Sociology Mind* 1 (2011): 130-7.

19   I. Shabane, M. Nkambwe and R. Chanda, "Landuse, Policy, and Squatter Settlements: The Case of Peri-Urban Areas in Botswana" *Applied Geography* 31 (2011): 677–86.

20   M. Nkambwe, "Contrasting Land Tenures: Subsistence Agriculture versus Urban Expansion on the Rural–Urban Fringe of Gaborone, Botswana" *International Development Planning Review* 25 (2003): 391-405; M. Nkambwe, "Customary Land Tenure Saves the Best Arable Aricultural Land in the Peri-Urban Zones of an African City: Gaborone, Botswana" *Applied Geography* 25 (2005).

21   A. Mosha "Low-Income Access to Urban Land and Housing in Botswana" *Urban Forum* 24 (2013); N. Batisani and O. Ranko, "The Geography of Despair: Urban Environmental Justice Through Income-Based Residential Zonation, Gaborone City, Botswana" *Journal of Urban and Environmental Engineering* 6 (2012).

22   Statistics Botswana, "Preliminary Results of the Botswana Core Welfare Indicators (Poverty) Survey 2009/10" Stats Brief No. 2011/15, Gaborone, 2011.

23   T. Ajilore and O. Yinusa "An Analysis of Employment Intensity of Sectoral Output Growth in Botswana" *Southern African Business Review* 15 (2012); H. Siphambe and M. Motswapong. "Female Participation in the Labour Market of Botswana: Results from the 2005/06 Labour Force Survey Data" *Botswana Journal of Economics* 7 (2011): 65-78.

24   Statistics Botswana, "Prelimary Results of the Botswana Core Welfare Indicators (Poverty) Survey" p. 5; Central Statistics Office (CSO). "Preliminary Labour Force Survey Results" Stats Brief No. 2006/02, Gaborone, 2006.

25   T. Gwebu, "Environmental Problems Among Low Income Urban Residents: An Empirical Analysis of Old Naledi-Gaborone, Botswana" *Habitat International* 27 (2003): 407-27.

26   A. Hovorka, "The Re(Production) of Gendered Positionality in Botswana's

Commercial Agricultural Sector" *Association of American Geographers* 95 (2005): 294-313.

27   J. Coates, A. Swindale and P. Bilinsky, "Household Food Insecurity Access Scale (HFIAS) for Measurement of Food Access: Indicator Guide (Version 3)" Food and Nutrition Technical Assistance Project, Academy for Educational Development, Washington, D.C., 2007.

28   A. Swindale and P. Bilinsky, "Household Dietary Diversity Score (HDDS) for Measurement of Household Food Access: Indicator Guide (Version 2)" Food and Nutrition Technical Assistance Project, Academy for Educational Development, Washington, D.C., 2006.

29   P. Bilinsky and A. Swindale, "Months of Adequate Household Food Provisioning (MAHFP) for Measurement of Household Food Access: Indicator Guide" Food and Nutrition Technical Assistance Project, Academy for Educational Development, Washington, D.C., 2007.

30   Central Statistics Office (CSO), *Botswana Demographic Survey* 2006 (Gaborone: Government Printer, 2009), p. 18.

31   Female-centred households are those with no husband/male partner in the household but can include relatives, children, and friends; male-centred households have no wife/female partner in the household but can include relatives, children, and friends; nuclear households have a husband/male partner and a wife/female partner with or without children; and extended families have a husband/male partner and a wife/female partner and children and relatives.

32   CSO, *Botswana Demographic Survey*, p. 96.

33   G. Mookodi, "We Are Struggling: Gender Dynamics of Survival in Low Income Households in Botswana" PhD Thesis, University of Toronto, 1999; G. Mookodi, "Male Violence Against Women in Botswana: A Discussion of Gender Uncertainties in a Rapidly Changing Environment" *African Sociological Review* 8 (2004): 118-38.

34   CSO, *Botswana Demographic Survey 2006*, p. 43. Only 4% of total migrants were aged 0-5 compared with 45% in the 15-34 age group.

35   M. van Klaveren, K. Tijdens, M. Hughie-Williams and N. Martin, "An Overview of Women's Work and Employment in Botswana" Country Report No. 5, Decisions for Life MDG 3 Project, Amsterdam Institute for Advanced Labour Studies, University of Amsterdam, 2009, p. 21.

36   Ibid.

37   B. Dodson, A. Chiweza and L. Riley, *Gender and Food Insecurity in Southern African Cities* AFSUN Urban Food Security Series No. 10, Cape Town, 2012.

38   T. Clausen, K. Charlton, K. Gobotswang and G. Holmboe-Ottesen, " Predictors of Food Variety and Dietary Diversity among Older Persons in Botswana" *Nutrition* 21 (2005): 86-95; S.Maruapula and K. Chapman-Novakofski, "Poor Intake of Milk, Vegetables, and Fruit with Limited Dietary Variety by Botswana's Elderly" *Journal of Nutrition for the Elderly* 25 (2006): 61–72; S. Maruapula and K. Chapman-Novakofski, "Health and Dietary Patterns of the Elderly in Botswana" 311-9; G. Tembwe, "Diet Diversity Coping Strategies and Food Access of Unemployed Young Single Mothers with Children under 9 Years of Age in Botswana" MA Thesis, UNISA, Pretoria 2010; S. Maruapula J. Jackson, J. Holsten, S. Shaibu, L. Malete, B. Wrotniak, S. Ratcliffe, G. Mokone, N. Stettler and C. Compher, "Socio-Economic Status and Urbanization are Linked to Snacks

and Obesity in Adolescents in Botswana" *Public Health Nutrition* 14 (2011): 2260-7; B. Wrotniak, L. Malete, S. Maruapula, J. Jackson, S. Shaibu, S. Ratcliffe, N. Stettler and C. Compher, "Association Between Socioeconomic Status Indicators and Obesity in Adolescent Students in Botswana, An African Country in Rapid Nutrition Transition" *Pediatric Obesity* 7(2012):e9-e13.

39   M. Nnyepi, "Household Factors are Strong Indicators of Children's Nutritional Status in Children with Access to Primary Health Care in the Greater Gaborone Area" *Scientific Research and Essays* 2 (2007): 55-61; O. Olesitse, "The Contribution of Cowpeas to Dietary Diversity and Food Access in Peri-Urban Gaborone, Botswana" MA Thesis, UNISA, Pretoria, 2010.

40   J. Crush and B. Frayne, "Supermarket Expansion and the Informal Food Economy in Southern African Cities: Implications for Urban Food Security" *Journal of Southern African Studies* 37 (2011): 781-807.

41   R. Emongor and J. Kirsten, "The Impact of South African Supermarkets on Agricultural Development in the SADC: A Case Study in Zambia, Namibia and Botswana" *Agrekon* 4 (2009): 60-84.

42   L. Durham, "Retail Across Borders: Choppies Brings Its Successful Botswana Supermarket Model to South Africa" *Supermarket & Retailer* May 2011.

43   K. Lane, A. Hovorka and A. Legwegoh,. "Urban Food Dynamics in Botswana: Insights from Gaborone's Central Business District" *African Geographical Review* 31 (2012): 111-25.

44   Ibid.

45   J. Crush, B. Frayne and M. McLachlan, *Rapid Urbanization and the Nutrition Transition in Southern Africa* AFSUN Urban Food Security Series No. 7, Cape Town, 2012; A. Legwegoh, "Urban Food Security in Gaborone, Botswana" PhD Thesis, University of Guelph, 2012.

46   Crush and Frayne, "Supermarket Expansion."

47   CSO, "2007 Informal Sector Survey Report" Central Statistics Office, Gaborone, 2009, p. 1

48   I. Obasi, B. Motshegwa and A. Mfundisi, "The State, Globalization and the Survival of the Urban Informal Sector in Botswana: The Challenge of Public Policy" *Africa Development* 33(2008): 55-79; F. Okurui and T. Botlhole, "Informal Financial Markets in Botswana: A Case Study of Gaborone City" *Development Southern Africa* 26 (2009): 255-70.

49   D. Keboneilwe and M. Madisa, "Policy Development and Implementation by MOA Botswana" Paper presented to Workshop on Urban Micro-Farming and HIV-AIDS, Johannesburg/Cape Town, 2005; T. Seleka, "Welfare Impacts of Import Controls on Botswana's Horticulture" *Agricultural Economics* 36 (2007): 305-11; M. Madisa and Y. Assefa. "Impact of Government Financial Incentives on Peri-Urban Vegetable Production in Botswana" *Journal of Horticulture and Forestry* 3 (2011): 264-9.

50   A. Mosha, "The Practice of Urban Agriculture in Gaborone" Department of Environmental Science, University of Botswana, Gaborone, 1999; A. Hovorka, "Urban Agriculture: Addressing Practical and Strategic Gender Needs" *Development in Practice* 16 (2006): 51-61.

51   A. Hovorka, "Exploring the Effects of Gender and Commercial (Peri-)Urban Agriculture Systems in Gaborone, Botswana" PhD Thesis,, Clark University,

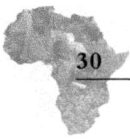

Worcester Mass., 2003; A. Hovorka, "Entrepreneurial Opportunities in Botswana: (Re)shaping Urban Agriculture Discourse" *Journal of Contemporary African Studies* 22 (2004): 367-88.

52   L. Sekwati, "Botswana: A Note on Economic Diversification" *Botswana Journal of Economics* 7 (2011): 79-85.

53   J. Crush, A. Hovorka and D. Tevera, "Food Security in Southern African Cities: The Place of Urban Agriculture" *Progress in Development Studies* 11 (2011): 285-305.

54   G. Letsedi, "Urban-Rural Linkages as an Urban Survival Strategy Among Urban Dwellers in Botswana: The Case of Broadhurst Residents" *Journal of Political Ecology* 10 (2003): 37-46; see also F Krüger, "Taking Advantage of Rural Assets as a Coping Strategy for the Urban Poor: The Case of Rural Urban Interrelations in Botswana" *Environment and Urbanization* 1 (1998): 119-34.

55   Ibid., p. 42.

56   B. Frayne, "Pathways of Food: Migration and Food Security in Southern African Cities" *International Development Planning Review* 32 (2010): 83-104.

57   P. Kebakile, "Rising Global Food Prices: Causes and Implications for Botswana" BIDPA Briefing, Botswana Institute for Development Policy Analysis, Gaborone, September 2008.

58   http://www.bhmarket.co.bw/bhm-content.php?cid=6

59   Botswana Agricultural Marketing Strategy (2011-2016) September 2011 at http://www.moa.gov.bw/downloads/botswana_agricultural_marketing_Strategy.pdf

60   Maruapula et al, "Socio-Economic Status and Urbanization are Linked to Snacks and Obesity."

www.ingramcontent.com/pod-product-compliance
Lightning Source LLC
Chambersburg PA
CBHW080135270326
41926CB00021B/4495